THIS BOOK BELONGS TO:

MONTHLY BILL TRACKER

MONTH OF: ____________________

EXPENSE/BILL	AMOUNT	DATE DUE	BALANCE	PAID

TOTAL MONTHLY EXPENSES: ______________________________

OTHER HOUSEHOLD EXPENSES

MONTH OF:____________________

EXPENSE/BILL	AMOUNT	DATE DUE	BALANCE	PAID

TOTAL EXPENSES:____________________________

MONTHLY BILL TRACKER

MONTH OF:____________________

EXPENSE/BILL	AMOUNT	DATE DUE	BALANCE	PAID

TOTAL MONTHLY EXPENSES:______________________________

OTHER HOUSEHOLD EXPENSES

MONTH OF: ____________________

EXPENSE/BILL	AMOUNT	DATE DUE	BALANCE	PAID

TOTAL EXPENSES: ______________________________

MONTHLY BILL TRACKER

MONTH OF: ____________________

EXPENSE/BILL	AMOUNT	DATE DUE	BALANCE	PAID

TOTAL MONTHLY EXPENSES: ______________________________

OTHER HOUSEHOLD EXPENSES

MONTH OF: ____________________

EXPENSE/BILL	AMOUNT	DATE DUE	BALANCE	PAID

TOTAL EXPENSES: ______________________________

MONTHLY BILL TRACKER

MONTH OF: ______________________

EXPENSE/BILL	AMOUNT	DATE DUE	BALANCE	PAID

TOTAL MONTHLY EXPENSES: ______________________________

OTHER HOUSEHOLD EXPENSES

MONTH OF: ______________________

EXPENSE/BILL	AMOUNT	DATE DUE	BALANCE	PAID

TOTAL EXPENSES: ______________________________

MONTHLY BILL TRACKER

MONTH OF: ____________________

EXPENSE/BILL	AMOUNT	DATE DUE	BALANCE	PAID

TOTAL MONTHLY EXPENSES: ____________________

OTHER HOUSEHOLD EXPENSES

MONTH OF: ____________________

EXPENSE/BILL	AMOUNT	DATE DUE	BALANCE	PAID

TOTAL EXPENSES: ______________________________

MONTHLY BILL TRACKER

MONTH OF: ____________________

EXPENSE/BILL	AMOUNT	DATE DUE	BALANCE	PAID

TOTAL MONTHLY EXPENSES: ____________________

OTHER HOUSEHOLD EXPENSES

MONTH OF: ____________________

EXPENSE/BILL	AMOUNT	DATE DUE	BALANCE	PAID

TOTAL EXPENSES: ______________________________

MONTHLY BILL TRACKER

MONTH OF: ____________________

EXPENSE/BILL	AMOUNT	DATE DUE	BALANCE	PAID

TOTAL MONTHLY EXPENSES: ______________________________

OTHER HOUSEHOLD EXPENSES

MONTH OF: ______________________

EXPENSE/BILL	AMOUNT	DATE DUE	BALANCE	PAID

TOTAL EXPENSES: ______________________

MONTHLY BILL TRACKER

MONTH OF:________________________

EXPENSE/BILL	AMOUNT	DATE DUE	BALANCE	PAID

TOTAL MONTHLY EXPENSES:____________________________________

OTHER HOUSEHOLD EXPENSES

MONTH OF: ______________________

EXPENSE/BILL	AMOUNT	DATE DUE	BALANCE	PAID

TOTAL EXPENSES: ______________________________

MONTHLY BILL TRACKER

MONTH OF: ____________________

EXPENSE/BILL	AMOUNT	DATE DUE	BALANCE	PAID

TOTAL MONTHLY EXPENSES: ____________________

OTHER HOUSEHOLD EXPENSES

MONTH OF: ____________________

EXPENSE/BILL	AMOUNT	DATE DUE	BALANCE	PAID

TOTAL EXPENSES: ______________________________

MONTHLY BILL TRACKER

MONTH OF: ____________________

EXPENSE/BILL	AMOUNT	DATE DUE	BALANCE	PAID

TOTAL MONTHLY EXPENSES: ______________________________

OTHER HOUSEHOLD EXPENSES

MONTH OF: ______________________

EXPENSE/BILL	AMOUNT	DATE DUE	BALANCE	PAID

TOTAL EXPENSES: ________________________________

MONTHLY BILL TRACKER

MONTH OF: ______________________

EXPENSE/BILL	AMOUNT	DATE DUE	BALANCE	PAID

TOTAL MONTHLY EXPENSES: ______________________________

OTHER HOUSEHOLD EXPENSES

MONTH OF: ____________________

EXPENSE/BILL	AMOUNT	DATE DUE	BALANCE	PAID

TOTAL EXPENSES: ______________________________

MONTHLY BILL TRACKER

MONTH OF: ____________________

EXPENSE/BILL	AMOUNT	DATE DUE	BALANCE	PAID

TOTAL MONTHLY EXPENSES: ____________________

OTHER HOUSEHOLD EXPENSES

MONTH OF:____________________

EXPENSE/BILL	AMOUNT	DATE DUE	BALANCE	PAID

TOTAL EXPENSES:____________________________

MONTHLY BILL TRACKER

MONTH OF:____________________

EXPENSE/BILL	AMOUNT	DATE DUE	BALANCE	PAID

TOTAL MONTHLY EXPENSES:____________________

OTHER HOUSEHOLD EXPENSES

MONTH OF: ____________________

EXPENSE/BILL	AMOUNT	DATE DUE	BALANCE	PAID

TOTAL EXPENSES: ______________________________

MONTHLY BILL TRACKER

MONTH OF: ______________________

EXPENSE/BILL	AMOUNT	DATE DUE	BALANCE	PAID

TOTAL MONTHLY EXPENSES: ______________________________

OTHER HOUSEHOLD EXPENSES

MONTH OF:___________________

EXPENSE/BILL	AMOUNT	DATE DUE	BALANCE	PAID

TOTAL EXPENSES:___________________

MONTHLY BILL TRACKER

MONTH OF:____________________

EXPENSE/BILL	AMOUNT	DATE DUE	BALANCE	PAID

TOTAL MONTHLY EXPENSES:____________________

OTHER HOUSEHOLD EXPENSES

MONTH OF: ____________________

EXPENSE/BILL	AMOUNT	DATE DUE	BALANCE	PAID

TOTAL EXPENSES: ______________________________

MONTHLY BILL TRACKER

MONTH OF: ______________________

EXPENSE/BILL	AMOUNT	DATE DUE	BALANCE	PAID

TOTAL MONTHLY EXPENSES: ______________________________

OTHER HOUSEHOLD EXPENSES

MONTH OF: ____________________

EXPENSE/BILL	AMOUNT	DATE DUE	BALANCE	PAID

TOTAL EXPENSES: ______________________________

MONTHLY BILL TRACKER

MONTH OF: ____________________

EXPENSE/BILL	AMOUNT	DATE DUE	BALANCE	PAID

TOTAL MONTHLY EXPENSES: ______________________________

OTHER HOUSEHOLD EXPENSES

MONTH OF:____________________

EXPENSE/BILL	AMOUNT	DATE DUE	BALANCE	PAID

TOTAL EXPENSES:____________________________

MONTHLY BILL TRACKER

MONTH OF: ____________________

EXPENSE/BILL	AMOUNT	DATE DUE	BALANCE	PAID

TOTAL MONTHLY EXPENSES: ______________________________

OTHER HOUSEHOLD EXPENSES

MONTH OF: ______________________

EXPENSE/BILL	AMOUNT	DATE DUE	BALANCE	PAID

TOTAL EXPENSES: ______________________

MONTHLY BILL TRACKER

MONTH OF: ____________________

EXPENSE/BILL	AMOUNT	DATE DUE	BALANCE	PAID

TOTAL MONTHLY EXPENSES: ______________________________

OTHER HOUSEHOLD EXPENSES

MONTH OF: ____________________

EXPENSE/BILL	AMOUNT	DATE DUE	BALANCE	PAID

TOTAL EXPENSES: ______________________________

MONTHLY BILL TRACKER

MONTH OF: ____________________

EXPENSE/BILL	AMOUNT	DATE DUE	BALANCE	PAID

TOTAL MONTHLY EXPENSES: ______________________________

OTHER HOUSEHOLD EXPENSES

MONTH OF:____________________

EXPENSE/BILL	AMOUNT	DATE DUE	BALANCE	PAID

TOTAL EXPENSES:____________________

MONTHLY BILL TRACKER

MONTH OF:________________________

EXPENSE/BILL	AMOUNT	DATE DUE	BALANCE	PAID

TOTAL MONTHLY EXPENSES:______________________________

OTHER HOUSEHOLD EXPENSES

MONTH OF:____________________

EXPENSE/BILL	AMOUNT	DATE DUE	BALANCE	PAID

TOTAL EXPENSES:____________________

MONTHLY BILL TRACKER

MONTH OF: ____________________

EXPENSE/BILL	AMOUNT	DATE DUE	BALANCE	PAID

TOTAL MONTHLY EXPENSES: ____________________

OTHER HOUSEHOLD EXPENSES

MONTH OF: ____________________

EXPENSE/BILL	AMOUNT	DATE DUE	BALANCE	PAID

TOTAL EXPENSES: ______________________________

MONTHLY BILL TRACKER

MONTH OF: ____________________

EXPENSE/BILL	AMOUNT	DATE DUE	BALANCE	PAID

TOTAL MONTHLY EXPENSES: ____________________

OTHER HOUSEHOLD EXPENSES

MONTH OF:____________________

EXPENSE/BILL	AMOUNT	DATE DUE	BALANCE	PAID

TOTAL EXPENSES:____________________

MONTHLY BILL TRACKER

MONTH OF: ______________________

EXPENSE/BILL	AMOUNT	DATE DUE	BALANCE	PAID

TOTAL MONTHLY EXPENSES: ______________________

OTHER HOUSEHOLD EXPENSES

MONTH OF: ______________________

EXPENSE/BILL	AMOUNT	DATE DUE	BALANCE	PAID

TOTAL EXPENSES: ________________________________

MONTHLY BILL TRACKER

MONTH OF: ____________________

EXPENSE/BILL	AMOUNT	DATE DUE	BALANCE	PAID

TOTAL MONTHLY EXPENSES: ______________________________

OTHER HOUSEHOLD EXPENSES

MONTH OF: ____________________

EXPENSE/BILL	AMOUNT	DATE DUE	BALANCE	PAID

TOTAL EXPENSES: ______________________________

MONTHLY BILL TRACKER

MONTH OF: ____________________

EXPENSE/BILL	AMOUNT	DATE DUE	BALANCE	PAID

TOTAL MONTHLY EXPENSES: ____________________

OTHER HOUSEHOLD EXPENSES

MONTH OF: ____________________

EXPENSE/BILL	AMOUNT	DATE DUE	BALANCE	PAID

TOTAL EXPENSES: ______________________________

MONTHLY BILL TRACKER

MONTH OF: ____________________

EXPENSE/BILL	AMOUNT	DATE DUE	BALANCE	PAID

TOTAL MONTHLY EXPENSES: ______________________________

OTHER HOUSEHOLD EXPENSES

MONTH OF: ____________________

EXPENSE/BILL	AMOUNT	DATE DUE	BALANCE	PAID

TOTAL EXPENSES: ______________________________

MONTHLY BILL TRACKER

MONTH OF:____________________

EXPENSE/BILL	AMOUNT	DATE DUE	BALANCE	PAID

TOTAL MONTHLY EXPENSES:____________________________

OTHER HOUSEHOLD EXPENSES

MONTH OF:____________________

EXPENSE/BILL	AMOUNT	DATE DUE	BALANCE	PAID

TOTAL EXPENSES:____________________________

MONTHLY BILL TRACKER

MONTH OF: ____________________

EXPENSE/BILL	AMOUNT	DATE DUE	BALANCE	PAID

TOTAL MONTHLY EXPENSES: ____________________

OTHER HOUSEHOLD EXPENSES

MONTH OF: ____________________

EXPENSE/BILL	AMOUNT	DATE DUE	BALANCE	PAID

TOTAL EXPENSES: ____________________

MONTHLY BILL TRACKER

MONTH OF: ____________________

EXPENSE/BILL	AMOUNT	DATE DUE	BALANCE	PAID

TOTAL MONTHLY EXPENSES: ____________________

OTHER HOUSEHOLD EXPENSES

MONTH OF:____________________

EXPENSE/BILL	AMOUNT	DATE DUE	BALANCE	PAID

TOTAL EXPENSES:____________________________

MONTHLY BILL TRACKER

MONTH OF:____________________

EXPENSE/BILL	AMOUNT	DATE DUE	BALANCE	PAID

TOTAL MONTHLY EXPENSES:____________________

OTHER HOUSEHOLD EXPENSES

MONTH OF: ____________________

EXPENSE/BILL	AMOUNT	DATE DUE	BALANCE	PAID

TOTAL EXPENSES: ______________________________

MONTHLY BILL TRACKER

MONTH OF: ______________________

EXPENSE/BILL	AMOUNT	DATE DUE	BALANCE	PAID

TOTAL MONTHLY EXPENSES: ______________________

OTHER HOUSEHOLD EXPENSES

MONTH OF: ____________________

EXPENSE/BILL	AMOUNT	DATE DUE	BALANCE	PAID

TOTAL EXPENSES: ____________________

MONTHLY BILL TRACKER

MONTH OF: ____________________

EXPENSE/BILL	AMOUNT	DATE DUE	BALANCE	PAID

TOTAL MONTHLY EXPENSES: ______________________________

OTHER HOUSEHOLD EXPENSES

MONTH OF: ______________________

EXPENSE/BILL	AMOUNT	DATE DUE	BALANCE	PAID

TOTAL EXPENSES: ______________________________

MONTHLY BILL TRACKER

MONTH OF: ____________________

EXPENSE/BILL	AMOUNT	DATE DUE	BALANCE	PAID

TOTAL MONTHLY EXPENSES: ________________________________

OTHER HOUSEHOLD EXPENSES

MONTH OF: ______________________

EXPENSE/BILL	AMOUNT	DATE DUE	BALANCE	PAID

TOTAL EXPENSES: ______________________

MONTHLY BILL TRACKER

MONTH OF: ____________________

EXPENSE/BILL	AMOUNT	DATE DUE	BALANCE	PAID

TOTAL MONTHLY EXPENSES: ______________________________

OTHER HOUSEHOLD EXPENSES

MONTH OF: ____________________

EXPENSE/BILL	AMOUNT	DATE DUE	BALANCE	PAID

TOTAL EXPENSES: ______________________________

MONTHLY BILL TRACKER

MONTH OF: ____________________

EXPENSE/BILL	AMOUNT	DATE DUE	BALANCE	PAID

TOTAL MONTHLY EXPENSES: ______________________________

OTHER HOUSEHOLD EXPENSES

MONTH OF: ____________________

EXPENSE/BILL	AMOUNT	DATE DUE	BALANCE	PAID

TOTAL EXPENSES: ______________________________

MONTHLY BILL TRACKER

MONTH OF: ____________________

EXPENSE/BILL	AMOUNT	DATE DUE	BALANCE	PAID

TOTAL MONTHLY EXPENSES: ______________________________

OTHER HOUSEHOLD EXPENSES

MONTH OF: ____________________

EXPENSE/BILL	AMOUNT	DATE DUE	BALANCE	PAID

TOTAL EXPENSES: ______________________________

MONTHLY BILL TRACKER

MONTH OF: ______________________

EXPENSE/BILL	AMOUNT	DATE DUE	BALANCE	PAID

TOTAL MONTHLY EXPENSES: ______________________

OTHER HOUSEHOLD EXPENSES

MONTH OF: ____________________

EXPENSE/BILL	AMOUNT	DATE DUE	BALANCE	PAID

TOTAL EXPENSES: ______________________________

MONTHLY BILL TRACKER

MONTH OF: ____________________

EXPENSE/BILL	AMOUNT	DATE DUE	BALANCE	PAID

TOTAL MONTHLY EXPENSES: ____________________

OTHER HOUSEHOLD EXPENSES

MONTH OF: ______________________

EXPENSE/BILL	AMOUNT	DATE DUE	BALANCE	PAID

TOTAL EXPENSES: ______________________________

MONTHLY BILL TRACKER

MONTH OF: ____________________

EXPENSE/BILL	AMOUNT	DATE DUE	BALANCE	PAID

TOTAL MONTHLY EXPENSES: ______________________________

OTHER HOUSEHOLD EXPENSES

MONTH OF: ____________________

EXPENSE/BILL	AMOUNT	DATE DUE	BALANCE	PAID

TOTAL EXPENSES: ______________________________

MONTHLY BILL TRACKER

MONTH OF:____________________

EXPENSE/BILL	AMOUNT	DATE DUE	BALANCE	PAID

TOTAL MONTHLY EXPENSES:____________________

OTHER HOUSEHOLD EXPENSES

MONTH OF: ______________________

EXPENSE/BILL	AMOUNT	DATE DUE	BALANCE	PAID

TOTAL EXPENSES: ______________________________

MONTHLY BILL TRACKER

MONTH OF: ____________________

EXPENSE/BILL	AMOUNT	DATE DUE	BALANCE	PAID

TOTAL MONTHLY EXPENSES: ______________________________

OTHER HOUSEHOLD EXPENSES

MONTH OF: ______________________

EXPENSE/BILL	AMOUNT	DATE DUE	BALANCE	PAID

TOTAL EXPENSES: ______________________________

MONTHLY BILL TRACKER

MONTH OF:____________________

EXPENSE/BILL	AMOUNT	DATE DUE	BALANCE	PAID

TOTAL MONTHLY EXPENSES:____________________

OTHER HOUSEHOLD EXPENSES

MONTH OF:____________________

EXPENSE/BILL	AMOUNT	DATE DUE	BALANCE	PAID

TOTAL EXPENSES:____________________

MONTHLY BILL TRACKER

MONTH OF: ____________________

EXPENSE/BILL	AMOUNT	DATE DUE	BALANCE	PAID

TOTAL MONTHLY EXPENSES: ______________________________

OTHER HOUSEHOLD EXPENSES

MONTH OF: ____________________

EXPENSE/BILL	AMOUNT	DATE DUE	BALANCE	PAID

TOTAL EXPENSES: ______________________________

MONTHLY BILL TRACKER

MONTH OF: ______________________

EXPENSE/BILL	AMOUNT	DATE DUE	BALANCE	PAID

TOTAL MONTHLY EXPENSES: ______________________________

OTHER HOUSEHOLD EXPENSES

MONTH OF:____________________

EXPENSE/BILL	AMOUNT	DATE DUE	BALANCE	PAID

TOTAL EXPENSES:____________________

MONTHLY BILL TRACKER

MONTH OF: ____________________

EXPENSE/BILL	AMOUNT	DATE DUE	BALANCE	PAID

TOTAL MONTHLY EXPENSES: ____________________

OTHER HOUSEHOLD EXPENSES

MONTH OF: ______________________

EXPENSE/BILL	AMOUNT	DATE DUE	BALANCE	PAID

TOTAL EXPENSES: ______________________________

MONTHLY BILL TRACKER

MONTH OF:______________________

EXPENSE/BILL	AMOUNT	DATE DUE	BALANCE	PAID

TOTAL MONTHLY EXPENSES:______________________________

OTHER HOUSEHOLD EXPENSES

MONTH OF: ______________________

EXPENSE/BILL	AMOUNT	DATE DUE	BALANCE	PAID

TOTAL EXPENSES: ______________________

MONTHLY BILL TRACKER

MONTH OF:____________________

EXPENSE/BILL	AMOUNT	DATE DUE	BALANCE	PAID

TOTAL MONTHLY EXPENSES:____________________

OTHER HOUSEHOLD EXPENSES

MONTH OF:________________________

EXPENSE/BILL	AMOUNT	DATE DUE	BALANCE	PAID

TOTAL EXPENSES:______________________________

MONTHLY BILL TRACKER

MONTH OF: ____________________

EXPENSE/BILL	AMOUNT	DATE DUE	BALANCE	PAID

TOTAL MONTHLY EXPENSES: ____________________

OTHER HOUSEHOLD EXPENSES

MONTH OF:____________________

EXPENSE/BILL	AMOUNT	DATE DUE	BALANCE	PAID

TOTAL EXPENSES:____________________________

MONTHLY BILL TRACKER

MONTH OF: ______________________

EXPENSE/BILL	AMOUNT	DATE DUE	BALANCE	PAID

TOTAL MONTHLY EXPENSES: ______________________

OTHER HOUSEHOLD EXPENSES

MONTH OF: ____________________

EXPENSE/BILL	AMOUNT	DATE DUE	BALANCE	PAID

TOTAL EXPENSES: ________________________________

MONTHLY BILL TRACKER

MONTH OF:____________________

EXPENSE/BILL	AMOUNT	DATE DUE	BALANCE	PAID

TOTAL MONTHLY EXPENSES:____________________________

OTHER HOUSEHOLD EXPENSES

MONTH OF: ____________________

EXPENSE/BILL	AMOUNT	DATE DUE	BALANCE	PAID

TOTAL EXPENSES: ______________________________

MONTHLY BILL TRACKER

MONTH OF: ____________________

EXPENSE/BILL	AMOUNT	DATE DUE	BALANCE	PAID

TOTAL MONTHLY EXPENSES: ____________________

OTHER HOUSEHOLD EXPENSES

MONTH OF:________________________

EXPENSE/BILL	AMOUNT	DATE DUE	BALANCE	PAID

TOTAL EXPENSES:__________________________________

Made in the USA
Middletown, DE
15 April 2020

88445135R00060